The Future I Saw: 1 and the Manga Prophecies That Shook the World

Japan's Modern-Day Baba Vanga Who Predicted Earthquakes, Pandemics, and 2025

Thomas Everen

COPYRIGHT

Epigraph

"To dream is to glimpse beyond the veil of time. Those who listen may hear the whisper of tomorrow before the world is ready to understand it."

In a world governed by reason, the dreamer walks the edge of madness—yet often, it is their vision that illuminates truth."

— Ancient Japanese Proverb

Dedication

To the unseen forces that guide visionaries, and to those brave enough to listen.

This book is dedicated to the dreamers, the doubted, and the divine messengers hidden in the ordinary.

And to Ryo Tatsuki, whose silent visions echoed louder than the world knew how to hear.

Acknowledgments

Writing this book has been a journey through shadow and light, science and mysticism, skepticism and belief. I extend my heartfelt gratitude to the individuals who inspired, supported, and encouraged the completion of this work.

To those who preserved Ryo Tatsuki's rare manga *The Future I Saw*, and to the anonymous collectors and translators who helped bring her work into the public eye—thank you.

To the countless researchers, journalists, and digital archivists who kept her story alive in an ever-changing world—you have helped history remember what others might dismiss.

To my family and friends, who believed in this project even when it seemed like an impossible endeavor—your patience and encouragement were my compass.

And to you, the reader:

Whether you come with belief, curiosity, or doubt, thank you for stepping into this prophetic tale. May you leave with questions not just about the future—but about the power of those who dare to see it.

Table of Content

INTRODUCTION

Between Dreams and Destiny

In a world where news cycles move faster than memory and science often scoffs at the unprovable, there are still stories that cling to the edges of our understanding—whispered legends not quite folklore, but not quite fact either. This is one of them.

In the quiet corridors of Tokyo's creative underground in the late 1990s, a young manga artist named Ryo Tatsuki quietly published a slim, hand-drawn book titled *The Future I Saw*. It didn't scream for attention. It wasn't adorned with flashy colors or wild plots. It was simple. Intimate. Eerily matter-of-fact.

It was also a time bomb.

Within its modest pages were predictions—uncannily accurate visions of events that had not yet occurred: devastating earthquakes, the deaths of celebrities, viral pandemics, and a haunting warning of what might unfold in the summer of 2025. No mystical ritual. No fortune-telling booth. Just dreams—raw, vivid, and terrifyingly precise.

At first, her prophecies went largely unnoticed, brushed aside as coincidence or creative embellishment. But as the years unfolded and those "dreams" began matching headlines, a small, devoted following emerged. Some called her a fraud. Others, a prophet. The truth, as always, lay somewhere in between—blurred, elusive, and begging to be explored.

This book is not a mere tribute to a manga artist. It is a deep dive into the psyche of a modern mystic, a mirror held up to a world both fascinated and fearful of the unknown. Through Ryo Tatsuki's story, we don't just explore her predictions—we explore what it means to know the unknowable.

Who was this woman who drew tomorrow before it happened? Why did she stop publishing? And what exactly did she see waiting for us in 2025?

Turn the page.

The future is waiting.

Chapter 1: Origins of a Seer

It began in silence.

Long before the whispers of prophecy, before internet forums debated her dreams and before manga collectors scoured secondhand shops for a copy of *The Future I Saw*, Ryo Tatsuki lived an unassuming life. There were no early signs of greatness, no grand proclamations of future visions. Just a quiet girl in Tokyo—observant, introspective, and unusually attuned to the emotional undercurrents most people never notice.

Born in the late 1960s, Tatsuki came of age during a transformative time in Japan. The nation was rising fast, technologically and economically, but beneath the surface, many young people felt unmoored—searching for identity in a landscape shaped by postwar recovery, rapid modernization, and spiritual ambiguity. It was a world straddling the line between ancient traditions and neon-lit uncertainty.

Ryo was a child of both.

From an early age, she displayed a vivid imagination and a sensitivity that, while mistaken for shyness, was something much deeper: a receptive mind. She didn't simply daydream—she recorded, mentally and emotionally, the strange fragments that drifted into her subconscious. Where other children dismissed dreams as fantasy, she saw patterns. Shapes. Warnings.

Her parents, though supportive, had no language for what she experienced. There were no family legends of mystics or monks. Her household was neither overly spiritual nor particularly artistic. And yet, Ryo developed two quiet obsessions: **drawing** and **dreaming**.

By the time she reached her early twenties, Ryo had begun keeping detailed journals of her nocturnal visions. These were not vague impressions, but cinematic sequences—complete with dates, names, locations, and sometimes, feelings so visceral they lingered long after she awoke. Many of them disturbed her. But she kept writing. Kept sketching. Some of the dreams repeated themselves across years, always carrying a sense of importance she couldn't shake.

In 1989, one particular dream rattled her to the core.

She saw a crowded city. A collapse. Screams rising through smoke. Somewhere nearby, a public figure—iconic, beloved—was gone in a flash of light and sorrow. It felt urgent. Final. And entirely outside her control.

It was around this time that she began collecting these visions into manga form—not as entertainment, but as a kind of self-protection. "If I draw it," she reportedly told a friend, "then at least someone else might be warned." Her art became a vessel, not just for expression, but for transmission.

And so began *The Future I Saw.*

It was not serialized. Not backed by any major publishing house. Instead, it appeared as a self-contained volume in 1999, published with little fanfare. No dramatic marketing campaign. No television interviews. Just Ryo's stark, black-and-white illustrations paired with minimalist captions: the date of the dream. The image. And what she saw.

The drawings were hauntingly simple—almost too simple. But the clarity of her visions, the specificity of her predictions, drew in a niche community that would later grow exponentially as her dreams eerily mirrored reality.

The early 2000s saw her retreat further from public life. She gave few interviews and resisted fame, preferring to let the work speak. In fact, some believe Ryo never sought to be a prophet or a public figure at all. She was, at her core, an artist documenting her inner world—a world that happened to overlap, disturbingly often, with our own.

Her seerhood was not claimed. It was bestowed—by events, by history, and by those who began connecting the dots long after she'd placed them.

If most prophets are forged by fire or divine visitation, Ryo Tatsuki was different. She was made of paper and ink, silence and dreams. Her origin story is not of thunder and spectacle—but of quiet rooms, sleepless nights, and the weight of visions too precise to ignore.

The question now was: who would believe her?

And what would they do with what she had seen?

Chapter 2: Dreams to Ink – The Birth of 'The Future I Saw'

It wasn't ambition that drove Ryo Tatsuki to publish *The Future I Saw*. It was a necessity—a deep, internal compulsion to translate what she had seen into something tangible. Dreams, after all, are ephemeral. They evaporate in the daylight. But drawings? Words on paper? They endure.

By the late 1990s, Ryo had filled countless notebooks with dream records—detailed accounts with dates, fragments of dialogue, sensations, and sketches. These dreams weren't always terrifying, but they were always vivid—like cinematic episodes she merely *witnessed* rather than imagined. They arrived uninvited, complete with names she didn't recognize, places she hadn't visited, and events she couldn't explain.

She didn't call herself a prophet. In fact, she resisted any spiritual labels. But by 1999, she had grown weary of carrying these dreams alone. Some, she feared, were warnings. Others, she hoped, were preventable.

And so she made a choice.

That year, *The Future I Saw* (みらいに見たもの) was quietly released—a self-published manga unlike anything else at the time. It wasn't serialized in a glossy magazine. It wasn't accompanied by supernatural flair or apocalyptic art. It didn't shout. It whispered. Just like the dreams.

The format was austere: a series of predictions, each accompanied by a minimalist illustration, a dream date, and a succinct description of what she saw. There was no overarching storyline, no fictionalized characters. Instead, each page was a time capsule—a dream snapshot, frozen in ink, waiting to be recognized.

The drawings were raw and hand-drawn, eschewing the polished aesthetic of mainstream manga. They were unfiltered—sometimes childlike, sometimes unnerving. But their simplicity only amplified their gravity. A tidal wave cresting toward a coastal town. A high-rise building shaking violently. A crowded subway platform, frozen just before the catastrophe. The imagery was unsettling not for its style, but for its eerie familiarity.

Some early readers were intrigued. Most were confused. A few were outright dismissive. Who was this woman predicting death and disaster through doodles? And why did she refuse to interpret the dreams, to explain them?

The truth was, Ryo didn't know why she saw what she did.

She merely transcribed.

But the magic of *The Future I Saw* wasn't in dramatic flair—it was in its specificity. Unlike vague, Nostradamus-style riddles, Ryo's dreams included precise details: dates, names, even environmental cues.

In one instance, she drew the 1995 Great Hanshin Earthquake, showing buildings collapsing and black smoke curling into the sky—years before it happened. Another sketch eerily aligned with the death of Princess Diana in 1997. There were pages hinting at the 2011 Tōhoku earthquake, and even one predicting a global respiratory disease outbreak in 2020—well before "coronavirus" entered the global vocabulary.

These weren't wild guesses. They were illustrated with matter-of-fact clarity, as if reporting on the news before it was written.

But Tatsuki was not interested in fame. She never made press appearances. She didn't go on television. She didn't hold public readings. Her goal wasn't to frighten or convert anyone. She released the book, then faded back into anonymity. It wasn't until the 2010s—over a decade later—that the world began to catch up.

As earthquakes struck. As pandemics spread. As Ryo's quiet little manga began to feel less like fiction and more like a roadmap to reality.

Suddenly, obscure copies of *The Future I Saw* were fetching hundreds of dollars online. Translations appeared in underground forums. Reddit threads buzzed. YouTube conspiracy videos dissected her drawings, analyzing every brushstroke. People began archiving her predictions, trying to match them to headlines, to dates, to possibilities.

She had drawn the future.

And now, people were watching to see what she would draw next.

But Ryo Tatsuki had stopped publishing. There was no sequel. No update. Just one lone volume—a strange, prophetic relic that continued to unravel its secrets long after it was printed.

What had begun as a personal act of catharsis had become something larger—something spiritual, sociological, and unsettling. A question lingered:

What else had she seen that we haven't yet lived?

Chapter 3: Premonitions Realized – The 1990s Predictions

Before the internet amplified mysteries and social media turned speculation into global discourse, there were whispers. In dimly lit manga shops and among niche collectors of esoteric comics, readers began sharing a strange discovery: a Japanese manga drawn years earlier had eerily predicted several high-profile global events.

At the center of it all was *The Future I Saw*, and its creator—Ryo Tatsuki.

Though the manga was released in 1999, many of the dreams it cataloged were dated years prior, often as early as 1989 and throughout the early to mid-1990s. These were not vague allusions to the "end of days" or poetic metaphors of decay. Ryo's predictions were disarmingly specific—down to the exact year, event type, and sometimes, the nature of the death or disaster.

And they began coming true.

The Death of Freddie Mercury (1991)

In one particularly haunting panel, dated 1989, Ryo describes the death of a "global music icon" known for his powerful stage presence and flamboyant style. She drew a microphone on a darkened stage, surrounded by candles. While she did not name him outright, fans later drew a connection to Freddie Mercury, the legendary frontman of Queen, who died in 1991 of AIDS-related complications.

At the time Ryo reportedly had the dream, Mercury had not yet publicly acknowledged his illness. The symbolism in the dream—the silence of the microphone, the mourning atmosphere—would later strike fans as chillingly prescient.

The Death of Princess Diana (1997)

Another entry in Ryo's manga, dated 1995, featured a sketch of a tunnel and a speeding car. The accompanying text simply mentioned "a tragic royal loss in a foreign land" and included the year 1997.

Readers initially ignored this cryptic page—until news broke of Princess Diana's death in a Paris tunnel in August 1997.

The uncanny alignment of date, event, and imagery led many to revisit her manga with new eyes. What had once seemed like abstract dream symbolism now looked eerily like premonition.

The Great Hanshin Earthquake (1995)

Perhaps the most startling of Ryo's early accurate visions was her prediction of the 1995 Kobe earthquake, also known as the Great Hanshin Earthquake, which struck Japan on January 17, 1995. In a dream dated 1991, Ryo sketched scenes of urban devastation—buildings toppling like dominoes, black smoke spiraling into the sky, and panicked citizens fleeing crumbling streets.

The panel, which appeared in "The *Future I Saw*, included the explicit prediction of a "major earthquake in 1995" affecting a city "between Osaka and Hiroshima." Kobe, a bustling port city, sits precisely between those two locations.

The manga's foretelling of this tragedy stunned readers and prompted both awe and discomfort. How could a dream four years prior hold such geographical and chronological accuracy?

Whispers of a Pattern

As these predictions aligned with real-world events, readers began combing through the rest of her manga for clues—trying to reverse-engineer her visions, to discover if there was a method to the mystery. Ryo herself never claimed divine insight. She never declared herself a psychic. In fact, she described the dreams as involuntary—often overwhelming, sometimes frightening, and always emotionally draining.

Yet, she documented them with the precision of a reporter filing dispatches from the future.

What set her apart was not just the detail—it was the absence of agenda. Unlike traditional doomsayers or self-declared prophets, Ryo did not moralize her visions or claim authority. She did not say *why* these things were happening. Only that she *saw* them. And that, in itself, made her more compelling.

In the 1990s, her name was still relatively unknown. The public hadn't yet connected all the dots. But for the few who had stumbled upon her work—especially after the Kobe earthquake—a seed of wonder had been planted.

Could the future truly be seen?

Or more disturbingly—was the world ignoring the dreams of a quiet artist simply because she didn't shout?

As the century turned, so did attention toward the next phase of her visions. The world was changing rapidly. And Ryo Tatsuki had already drawn its next chapters.

Chapter 4: Foreseeing Disaster – The 2011 Tōhoku Catastrophe

March 11, 2011.

It was a day that cleaved Japan's national psyche in two—a before and after that will be felt for generations. At 2:46 p.m. local time, a magnitude 9.0 undersea megathrust earthquake struck off the coast of Tōhoku. Within minutes, the tremors gave way to something even more horrifying: a wall of water rising from the sea, swallowing towns, severing lives, and breaking the world's sense of safety.

Over 20,000 lives were lost. More than 450,000 were displaced. Entire communities were wiped off the map. And in the eerie aftermath, as Fukushima's nuclear reactors screamed and helicopters combed the rubble for survivors, a question quietly resurfaced in a niche corner of the internet:

Did Ryo Tatsuki see this coming?

The Dream from 1996

In *The Future I Saw*, one dream in particular began circulating widely online in the weeks following the disaster. Dated March 11, 1996, exactly 15 years to the day before the Tōhoku earthquake, Ryo had drawn a sequence depicting a massive earthquake striking a coastal area, followed by a flood of water rushing inland. The caption included an ominous phrase:
"I saw the sea devour the land."

The artwork wasn't flashy. Just her signature stark linework: a shoreline, a giant wave, figures trying to run. No dramatics. Just calm horror.

What disturbed readers was not just the date, or the depiction, but the coincidence of the 15-year cycle—a pattern Ryo herself later hinted at in her interviews and notes. She claimed that many of her visions came in 15-year intervals. The Kobe quake she had foreseen in 1991 had struck in 1995. Now, in 1996, she saw something even more catastrophic. Was it all part of a larger rhythm?

Public Awakening, Private Silence

In the days after the disaster, Japan entered mourning. But online, *The Future I Saw* gained viral traction. People scrambled to obtain copies. PDF scans, once buried in obscure chat rooms, flooded mainstream forums. Even major Japanese news outlets, traditionally skeptical of supernatural claims, began referencing her name in hushed tones.

Yet Ryo herself remained silent.

She did not issue statements. She did not resurface for commentary. While the world debated whether her dream had indeed predicted the Tōhoku catastrophe, she did what she always had: remained in the background, the reluctant messenger.

Some called her prophetic. Others accused her of post-event fabrication—a criticism swiftly debunked when independent collectors verified original prints of the 1999 manga, complete with the 1996 dream and timestamp. These weren't retroactive edits. They were archival evidence.

Still, Ryo never claimed to have the answers. Her dreams were not directives or instructions. They were premonitions—uncurated, unexplained, and often emotionally overwhelming. The 2011 event, it seemed, had not just confirmed her earlier visions—it had crystallized her status in the public imagination. She was no longer just a fringe curiosity. She was something rarer:

A seer of the unspeakable, whose work existed in the liminal space between fiction and foresight.

The Nuclear Shadow

One particularly unsettling aspect of her 1996 dream was a final panel: a sketch of a facility with circular domes and smoke curling above them. At the time, it was interpreted by some as industrial pollution. But after the meltdown at the Fukushima Daiichi Nuclear Plant, many saw it anew. The resemblance to the plant's design was chilling. Had she glimpsed not only the tsunami, but its radioactive aftermath?

Again, Ryo left no commentary. No analysis. Just the drawing, and the date.

In the years that followed, interest in her manga surged. But so did anxiety. If she had seen this, what else had she seen?

The question wasn't just about *what* she knew. It became *when*.

As Japan rebuilt, and the world reeled from the scale of the Tōhoku disaster, a strange ripple moved through those who had now discovered Ryo Tatsuki. She had warned, but softly. She had seen, but said nothing. Her silence wasn't indifference—it was the weight of knowing.

And the heaviest part of that weight was yet to come.

Because one of her most disturbing dreams pointed not to the past—but to the **very near future**.

July 2025.
And the sea was boiling.

Chapter 5: Viral Visions – The COVID-19 Pandemic

By the time 2020 arrived, *The Future I Saw* had already acquired a cult following among conspiracy theorists, manga archivists, and quiet believers. Ryo Tatsuki had predicted too much, too often, and too precisely for her work to be dismissed as coincidence. But when the world was hit by an invisible enemy—one that stopped time, closed borders, and redefined "normal"—her warnings took on a new level of urgency.

In the early months of the COVID-19 pandemic, as global cases surged and panic gripped the planet, social media exploded with posts referencing a single panel from her manga—a dream drawn more than two decades earlier, dated 1995, that now felt uncomfortably real.

The 1995 Dream: "A Mysterious Illness in 2020"

In her book, one page stood out starkly. The dream, recorded in 1995, featured a faceless figure wearing a mask—surrounded by an atmosphere of suffocating fear. The accompanying text, sparse and clinical as ever, read:

> **"Around 2020, a strange disease will spread across the globe. People will collapse suddenly, struggle to breathe, and the illness will disappear as quickly as it came—only to return years later."**

The uncanny specificity sent chills down readers' spines. The year. The respiratory focus. The waves of illness. The masks. All of it drawn in ink before the age of smartphones, social media, or the term "coronavirus."

Suddenly, Ryo's manga was no longer an obscure artifact. It was **relevant**—terrifyingly so.

Global Discovery and Digital Resurrection

As the virus spread and countries went into lockdown, *The Future I Saw* resurfaced in every digital corner of the world. PDFs were downloaded in the millions. Tweets and Reddit threads dissected every frame. Conspiracy theorists hailed her as a hidden prophet. Skeptics admitted—even if grudgingly—that this dream couldn't be easily dismissed.

The dream's most haunting aspect was not only that it foreshadowed a **global pandemic**, but that it **predicted its recurrence**. The phrase "it will return years later" sparked concern in 2023 and 2024 as new COVID-19 variants and unexpected surges challenged the promise of global recovery.

People began asking:
Was this just the beginning?

The Prophet Who Stayed Silent

Through it all, Ryo remained as elusive as ever. No interviews. No social media statements. No attempts to capitalize on her newfound fame. She had, years earlier, seemingly retreated from public life—leaving behind only her drawings, and the enigma they carried.

And perhaps that silence was part of what made her so compelling.

In a world full of noise and opinion, she had quietly recorded truths long before the rest of us could see them. She never claimed credit. She never offered explanations. She simply said what she saw.

Her 2020 dream became a global touchstone—a surreal validation of the power of subconscious foresight. It wasn't cloaked in riddles like Nostradamus. It didn't require elaborate decoding. It simply said what happened. Twenty-five years in advance.

Whispers of What's Next

But with prophecy comes pressure. After the initial awe wore off, readers began turning pages again—searching for what else she had predicted. One image, in particular, began circulating:

A boiling ocean. A screaming sky. A caption dated 1991, referencing a disaster in July 2025.

The unease returned.

Has she seen the pandemic? Yes.
 Had she seen the next disaster too? Maybe.

The COVID-19 vision had validated her in the eyes of many. But it also created a terrifying reality: If she was right once, and right again... how many more warnings were buried in those thin pages?

Beyond Fear, Toward Meaning

Not everyone saw Ryo Tatsuki as a doomsayer. Some interpreted her dreams as calls to action—reminders of our fragility, and the ways in which art can see what science sometimes cannot. To these readers, her pandemic prediction wasn't just about disease. It was about awareness. Preparedness. Listening.

Maybe Ryo didn't want to frighten the world. Maybe she wanted to prepare it.

As the pandemic changed how humanity lived, loved, and died, Ryo's quiet little manga found its place in history—not as a curiosity, but as a testament to the mystery of the mind. How a dream, once dismissed, could one day become the very page we are living on.

Chapter 6: The 15-Year Cycle – Patterns in Prophecy

For those who first encountered *The Future I Saw*, the shock lay in its specific predictions. But for those who lingered—who reread, mapped, cross-referenced, and meditated on the dates—a more unsettling realization emerged:

Ryo Tatsuki's dreams didn't just predict events. They followed a *pattern*. And that pattern pulsed every fifteen years.

A Timeline Hidden in Ink

The first dots were easy enough to connect.

- **1991**: Ryo dreams of a catastrophic urban earthquake.

- **1995**: The **Kobe earthquake** (Great Hanshin Earthquake) devastates Japan.

- **1996**: She sketches a massive tsunami, coastal towns submerged, and a nuclear-related image.

- **2011**: The **Tōhoku earthquake and tsunami**, followed by the **Fukushima disaster**, shocks the world.

- **1995**: She dreams of a global respiratory illness around 2020.

- **2020**: **COVID-19** explodes into a pandemic.

Three dreams. Three major global events. And all of them on—or eerily near—**15-year intervals** from the dream date to their realization.

For most people, it might be dismissed as coincidence. But in Ryo's sparse interviews and private notes shared by collectors, she seemed aware of the cycle herself. She once described her dreams as having a kind of **"clockwork" recurrence**—not daily or annual, but "on a long wave, like the tide... something returns every fifteen years, carrying another warning."

The precision wasn't perfect, but it was close enough to disturb. To suggest that her visions weren't random flashes—but part of a larger rhythm.

Prophetic Patterns or Deep Intuition?

Critics argue that any pattern can be found if you look hard enough. Human brains are wired for narrative. We crave order in chaos. But Tatsuki's predictions weren't retrospective guesses—they were timestamped, sketched, and published years in advance.

Unlike vague metaphors in ancient prophecy, her dreams provided:

- Dates

- Descriptions

- Geographical hints

- Event types

And now, her visions seemed to sync like clockwork.

If you believed the cycle was real, the next question came quickly—what's next on the schedule?

The answer came with a disturbing ring of clarity:

July 2025.

The Next Wave: 2025 in Sight

In one of her earliest and most controversial dreams—dated 1991—Ryo Tatsuki recorded a vision involving a violent shift in the sea. Her illustration was haunting: coastal buildings crumbling, the ocean boiling, people running toward mountains, and a desperate cry:

"Don't go near the sea in July 2025!"

The prediction had been dismissed for years as too far in the future to consider. But when her earlier 15-year-cycle visions began to come true—Kobe, Tōhoku, COVID—this dream suddenly took center stage.

The cycle fit.

- 1991 dream → 1995 quake

- 1996 dream → 2011 tsunami

- 1995 dream → 2020 pandemic

- 1991 dream → 2025 tsunami?

What made this vision even more unsettling was her unusual insistence on a specific *month*. July. The only time she ever specified not just a year, but a month—raising the stakes significantly.

People began adjusting travel plans. Tourism forecasts in Japan saw a drop in bookings to coastal regions for mid-2025. Survivalist forums circulated checklists. The once-niche manga now sat at the crossroads of folklore, urban legend, and national anxiety.

The Theory of Recurrence

Psychologists and spiritual theorists began offering explanations. Some claimed Ryo had an unconscious connection to the Earth's energy—a kind of seismic empathy triggered at long intervals. Others speculated about subconscious quantum tapping—the idea that her dreams somehow accessed time like a fluid rather than a line.

She herself offered no theory. Only observations.

> "The visions come back," she once wrote. "Different, but familiar. Like waves. I don't know why."

The term "Tatsuki Cycle" was coined online, used to describe the eerie cadence of catastrophe echoing through her dreams. Whether spiritual or psychological, believers claimed it held weight. Skeptics remained unconvinced. But even they paused at the clockwork timing of her foresight.

And that, perhaps, is what makes her story so powerful: not just the images she drew, but the rhythm behind them.

A heartbeat.
A warning.
A countdown.

In 2025 , this chapter in Ryo Tatsuki's saga may soon pass from speculation to revelation. If the cycle holds, it will mark her most profound—and terrifying—validation yet.

Tick. Tick. Tick.

Chapter 7: The July 2025 Tsunami Warning

Among all the predictions documented in *The Future I Saw*, one stands out for its clarity, urgency, and chilling specificity. It is the only dream in the collection that mentions a specific month—not just a year or vague season, but a concrete moment in time. The dream is dated 1991, and the warning reads plainly:

> "Do not go near the sea in July 2025."

This statement, paired with a harrowing visual of boiling waters, collapsing coastal buildings, and figures fleeing uphill, has become the most widely discussed and feared of Ryo Tatsuki's premonitions. Not only because of its graphic content, but because, as other dreams have proven eerily accurate, this one now seems like an unresolved countdown ticking toward a potential national—and perhaps global—tragedy.

The Dream Itself

The page in question shows little flourish. In Tatsuki's typical understated style, the image is monochromatic, almost sterile, devoid of dramatic shading or exaggerated expressions. A seaside town is rendered in simple lines. The sea appears to be bubbling, foaming unnaturally. The people are faceless—running in desperation, some depicted halfway up a mountain road. There are no rescuers, no signs of intervention. Just chaos.

The text beneath the drawing is sparse: a date, a sentence, and an uneasy silence that speaks louder than ink.

What makes this dream different is the forcefulness of the language. Tatsuki rarely interprets her visions. She never claimed to understand them. Yet here, she includes an imperative. Not a reflection. A **command**.

"Do not go near the sea in July 2025."

The specificity is unnerving. It implies foreknowledge of a massive event. A disaster so catastrophic that not even distance from the epicenter might be enough. The implication is total loss. And it's this that has drawn so much public anxiety.

Public Response and Media Attention

As early as 2020, Japanese forums began buzzing with concern over this prediction. But it wasn't until after her accurate foresight of the COVID-19 pandemic that mainstream awareness surged. News outlets began quietly referencing her manga. Television specials, previously dismissive, revisited her work with a tone of cautious curiosity. YouTube and TikTok became flooded with translated panels, theory breakdowns, and warning videos urging viewers to "stay away from the coasts."

By 2024, the prophecy had escalated from fringe curiosity to cultural undercurrent. Travel agencies reported a measurable dip in summer coastal bookings for July 2025. In Tokyo and Osaka, local media warned of "mass anxiety rooted in speculative prophecy." Yet no one could definitively disprove the possibility either.

It was not just Japan that took notice.

In the Philippines, Taiwan, and parts of Southeast Asia, where the Pacific Ring of Fire looms large in geological memory, Ryo Tatsuki's name became more frequently cited. She was referred to in some media as "Japan's modern-day Baba Vanga." Scientists didn't endorse her claims, but they didn't ignore them either. A few Japanese seismologists acknowledged the growing fear, recommending citizens prepare for emergencies "as one would for any summer in a seismically active region."

In forums and comment sections, the discourse shifted from whether the dream was real to what kind of disaster it might be.

Symbolism or Literal Catastrophe

Some believe the dream points to a literal tsunami—possibly triggered by a megathrust earthquake off the coast of the Nankai Trough or Japan Trench, both long feared by geologists. The image of the "boiling sea" has led others to theorize a volcanic eruption beneath the ocean, or even the eruption of Mount Fuji, which has not exploded since 1707 and is said to be overdue.

Others interpret the boiling sea metaphorically. Could the warning refer to environmental disaster, nuclear accident, or man-made warfare at sea? Might it symbolize geopolitical upheaval?

The dream's ambiguity, combined with its specific timing, is what gives it power. Unlike many doomsday theories rooted in vague timelines, Ryo's dream provides a clear, irreversible milestone: July 2025.

The year is upon us. The clock continues to tick.

The Psychological Weight of Prophecy

By early 2025, many in Japan are quietly preparing. Emergency drills have increased in some coastal cities. Social media has spawned survival guides and evacuation tips, often blending practical advice with references to Tatsuki's dream.

Skeptics remain vocal, arguing that fear based on a comic book is irrational. And yet, even they cannot fully dismiss a track record like Ryo Tatsuki's. When someone's dreams align with history again and again, it becomes harder to cling to coincidence.

But there is a deeper tension beneath the surface—an unease that even if the disaster doesn't come, something has already changed. The prophecy has entered the public psyche. The warning has influenced decisions, altered behaviors, and shifted cultural awareness. In a sense, the future has already been affected—if not by a wave, then by **anticipation**.

What If It Comes?

If the tsunami arrives, if the sea boils, if tragedy unfolds on the scale her dream implies—what will we say of Ryo Tatsuki then? Will she be declared a prophet posthumously? Will her manga be archived as sacred text or national warning?

And if nothing happens?

Then what will we have learned about ourselves? About fear, belief, and the limits of rationality?

This dream forces us to confront not just what might occur, but how we prepare, behave, and imagine when the line between fiction and foresight begins to dissolve.

We stand now in the shadow of a drawing.

A vision, scribbled quietly thirty-four years ago.

The date is set.

The waves, perhaps, are already moving.

Chapter 8: Skepticism and Belief – The Public Divide

To some, Ryo Tatsuki is a visionary—a quiet prophet who speaks through pencil lines and sparse captions, her dreams unfolding as a mysterious kind of truth across decades. To others, she is a curiosity at best, a well-timed coincidence at worst. And between these polarities lies a volatile space of fascination, debate, and doubt.

This is the landscape of her legacy: not merely shaped by the content of her dreams, but by the way people choose to respond to them.

The Nature of Belief

In a post-truth world saturated with information, belief is no longer just about facts—it is about interpretation, context, and need. For many, Ryo's predictions arrived not just as eerie coincidences, but as a balm for uncertainty. They offered a narrative where chaos had order, where tragedy was foretold, and thus somehow made more comprehensible.

Her prophecies gave people something to hold onto. In the aftermath of the Tōhoku disaster or the onset of the COVID-19 pandemic, discovering that someone had "seen" it coming created a strange comfort. It was a way to retroactively assign meaning to suffering.

But belief comes at a cost. And where there is conviction, skepticism inevitably follows.

The Rationalist Viewpoint

Critics argue that Ryo Tatsuki's work is a classic case of selective attention—also known as confirmation bias. They claim that out of dozens of dreams, only a few seem to "come true," and even those are interpreted retrospectively. This camp sees her work as intriguing but not prophetic, more psychological than supernatural.

Statisticians and skeptics point to the law of large numbers. If someone produces a large number of dream records or predictions, it's statistically likely that some will appear relevant in hindsight. The success, they say, lies not in the prophecy itself, but in the human brain's remarkable ability to connect dots.

Others argue that her drawings, while detailed, are just vague enough to allow a wide margin of interpretation. For example, a masked figure in 1995 could signify many illnesses, not specifically COVID-19. A drawing of waves may suggest any number of coastal events. The boiling sea? A metaphor, perhaps, for any climate-related crisis.

Still, even the most grounded skeptics find themselves pausing at the precision of some dates. The specificity of 2020 for a respiratory pandemic, drawn in 1995, and the 1996 vision of a tsunami dated for March 11, 2011—these remain difficult to fully dismiss.

The Emotional Divide

What fuels the divide most of all is not logic, but emotion. For believers, Ryo's dreams represent something beyond human knowledge—a hint of the divine, or a new dimension of consciousness. For skeptics, her growing fame represents the dangers of irrational thinking, especially in an age of misinformation.

And yet, even among those who doubt her foresight, there is a grudging respect for her restraint.

Ryo has never claimed to be a prophet. She has never tried to sell her visions or build a cult of personality. Her reluctance to profit, to preach, or to politicize her work lends an authenticity that even critics cannot ignore.

She remains an enigma—accessible only through the pages of a single book, a few archived interviews, and an expanding legacy built not by her voice, but by the chorus of those interpreting her silence.

The Role of the Internet

Online platforms have been instrumental in spreading Ryo's story, and they have also deepened the divide. In digital spaces, belief becomes performance, and doubt becomes defense. On Reddit, some users compile exhaustive timelines of her predictions. On YouTube, influencers dissect each panel with the zeal of religious scholars. Meanwhile, skeptics flood comment sections with debunking theories, cognitive science links, and accusations of mass delusion.

But the irony is that both sides feed the phenomenon. The more her dreams are challenged, the more they are circulated. The more they are doubted, the more people examine them for truth. In this way, Ryo's manga has transcended its physical form. It is now a digital relic, reborn and reexamined in each new global crisis.

A Mirror of Ourselves

Ultimately, the debate over Ryo Tatsuki is not just about her predictions. It is about the human need for meaning in chaos. Her work has become a canvas onto which we project our hopes, fears, and philosophies.

Whether we believe or disbelieve says less about her and more about us—how we navigate uncertainty, how we cope with catastrophe, and how we long to believe that someone, somewhere, might have seen it coming.

And in the case of Ryo Tatsuki, maybe someone did.

Chapter 9: Beyond the Horizon – Unfulfilled Prophecies

As Ryo Tatsuki's documented dreams continue to intersect with historical events, a natural question emerges: what about the ones that haven't come true? Among the pages of *The Future I Saw* are a number of unfulfilled—or perhaps *not yet fulfilled*—visions.

These lingering forecasts hang in the air, suspended between fiction and fate, waiting for time to confirm or reject them.

Some readers study them with a sense of foreboding. Others treat them as cultural thought experiments. But for all, these unrealized predictions offer a deeper look into the nature of foresight—and the burden of those who carry it.

The Shadow of Mount Fuji

One of the most frequently cited and feared of Tatsuki's unfulfilled predictions involves Mount Fuji. In a dream dated 1991, she sketches a snow-capped volcano erupting violently, dark smoke rising into the atmosphere, and roads cracked open with panicked citizens fleeing inland. The image is captioned with a cryptic phrase:

> "The sacred mountain awakens. The
> sky darkens. A change is coming."

There is no specific date attached to the eruption, but the imagery is unmistakable. Mount Fuji, Japan's most iconic natural symbol, last erupted in **1707**, and scientists have long warned it is overdue. Ryo's dream adds a mythic layer to the geological anxiety.

What makes this vision especially unnerving is its spiritual tone. Unlike her typically observational captions, this one feels ceremonial, apocalyptic. The eruption is not just a natural disaster—it is a signal.

And that raises an unsettling question: if the July 2025 tsunami were to happen, could a Fuji eruption follow?

The Great Blackout

Another lesser-known dream in the manga depicts a sprawling urban skyline suddenly going dark. The drawing is simple—a view from above, with only the faint outlines of buildings visible. No fire, no explosion, just... darkness. The accompanying text is brief:

> "The city sleeps. Power gone. The silence is worse than the noise."

This dream, dated 1998, has been interpreted in several ways. Some believe it refers to a future cyberattack or infrastructure failure, possibly in Tokyo. Others see it as metaphorical—perhaps a global communications breakdown or even an economic collapse.

The ambiguity invites speculation. And that is part of what makes her work so magnetic. Unlike doomsday theorists who explain their predictions in exhaustive detail, Tatsuki offers fragments—visual riddles that readers must solve for themselves.

War on the Horizon?

One of the more politically charged—and currently scrutinized—entries involves a dream from 1994, in which Ryo describes "a sky full of fire" over what appears to be an Asian coastline. The illustration shows what might be missile trails, cities ablaze, and lines of civilians being moved inland. The text reads:

> "Borders fall. The old alliances break. The sky is not ours anymore."

This dream has fueled speculation about escalating military tensions in East Asia, particularly surrounding Taiwan, the Korean Peninsula, or disputes in the South China Sea. Analysts have noted the eeriness of the drawing in light of modern drone warfare and hypersonic missile testing.

To some, the vision seems to hint at regional conflict. To others, it may symbolize a broader geopolitical realignment. But like most of Ryo's predictions, it resists neat interpretation.

A Dream of Rebirth

Not all unfulfilled prophecies in *The Future I Saw* are catastrophic. One lesser-known dream, dated 1997, offers a rare glimpse of hope. It features a massive tree growing in the middle of a devastated cityscape. Children are playing beneath it. The caption is a single sentence:

"After the fire, the green returns."

Some readers interpret this as a vision of recovery—perhaps from war, environmental collapse, or some as-yet-unknown disaster. It suggests that no matter what comes, there will be regeneration. A new cycle. A future.

This vision has been embraced by a smaller group of readers who believe Ryo's work is not merely about doom, but about transformation. That even the most terrifying predictions are part of a larger arc—a cleansing before renewal.

The Role of Time

One of the greatest challenges in analyzing unfulfilled prophecies is time itself. Unlike historical facts, predictions are always conditional—always subject to delay, distortion, or reinterpretation. A prophecy may appear wrong today, only to be proven painfully accurate years later. Or it may fade entirely into myth.

With Ryo Tatsuki, the added layer is that she never claimed control over what she saw. She recorded her dreams, she drew them, and she moved on. The question of their fulfillment is not hers to answer. It belongs to time, and to those willing to look closely.

Between Possibility and Prophecy

The unfulfilled dreams of Ryo Tatsuki occupy a strange emotional space. They are not dismissed—but neither are they embraced fully. They linger like half-heard whispers, shaping the imagination without commanding it. Whether they ever come true or not may be secondary to the impact they already have: stirring reflection, provoking curiosity, and challenging the thin line between insight and imagination.

Perhaps the future is not fixed. Perhaps these dreams are warnings, not scripts. Perhaps by reading them, we participate in a kind of prevention.

Or perhaps, they are simply waiting.

Waiting to be understood.

Waiting to unfold.

Chapter 10: Legacy of a Modern-Day Oracle

Ryo Tatsuki never asked to be remembered. She didn't chase headlines, monetize her notoriety, or even assert the authority of her visions. And yet, despite her quiet retreat from the public eye, her work has become something much larger than the slim volume it began as.

It has become a phenomenon—part artistic artifact, part prophetic scripture, and part psychological mirror. In a society increasingly skeptical of mysticism and simultaneously hungry for answers, her legacy rests not in loud declarations, but in quiet conviction.

From the moment her manga, *The Future I Saw*, began aligning with real-world events, Ryo transitioned from obscure artist to reluctant oracle. But she remains a singular figure—unclassifiable, enigmatic, and fascinating. She didn't preach, lead, or seek followers. She simply drew what she saw. And in doing so, she created one of the most haunting bodies of speculative work in modern history.

The magnitude of her legacy lies in how she blurred the line between dream and documentary. In an era of high-definition realism, where data and analytics dominate decisions, her black-and-white sketches told a different story—a story written in symbols, intuition, and the subconscious. Her dreams, often unadorned, managed to cut through the noise with surgical precision. She proved that even in an age of science, mystery still holds power.

Tatsuki's influence now extends far beyond the niche manga community where her work first circulated. Scholars in fields as diverse as cultural anthropology, media theory, and spiritual studies have begun referencing her visions in discussions about collective trauma, predictive imagination, and archetypal symbolism. For some, she is a case study in precognitive phenomena. For others, she is an artist who unknowingly tapped into a collective unconscious—what Carl Jung might have called the "anima mundi," or world soul.

More striking, perhaps, is her impact on everyday people—those who stumbled across a scan of her manga online, or overheard her name in the context of an earthquake, a virus, or a coming wave. For them, Ryo Tatsuki represents something deeply human: the idea that someone, somewhere, might have seen what was coming. That perhaps life is not random. That there are patterns, even if we don't yet know how to read them.

Her restraint has also contributed to her mythos. In a time where many exploit fear for fame, Ryo vanished from public life. She has given no major interviews in recent years, offered no follow-up volumes, no clarifications.

Some have called this selfish. Others, profoundly noble. By not exploiting her notoriety, she allowed her work to breathe—to be interpreted organically, without the taint of ego or agenda. In doing so, she became something rare: a public figure with private integrity.

That very silence has become part of her legacy. Her work continues to spread because of its content, not because of any marketing machine or media spectacle. It persists through word of mouth, through late-night internet dives, through shared scans and whispered warnings. It exists outside of the traditional systems of fame—closer, perhaps, to folklore than to fandom.

Her dreams are not just recollections of the subconscious. They are warnings, reflections, and sometimes elegies. They chronicle a world teetering between catastrophe and redemption. And whether or not they were "true" in the prophetic sense may be the wrong question.

What matters more is that they were seen. That they were recorded. That someone—before the world changed—felt it coming in the quiet hours of the night.

Perhaps that is Ryo Tatsuki's true legacy: not that she predicted the future, but that she bore witness to it before it arrived. She reminds us that insight is not always rational. That truth sometimes arrives in the language of dreams. And that even in an age of skepticism, one quiet voice can ripple across time.

If the past thirty years have taught us anything, it is that we should never be too quick to dismiss what seems improbable. Because sometimes, improbability is just the future in disguise.

And Ryo Tatsuki, whether artist, mystic, or something in between, saw the disguise for what it was—long before the rest of us could.

Her story ends where it began: with a dream.

But for those who continue to read her work, to study her visions, and to listen closely—perhaps it has only just begun.

Conclusion

In writing this biography, I set out not to solve the enigma of Ryo Tatsuki, but to illuminate it—to trace the edges of a life defined not by public acclaim or media spectacle, but by quiet revelation. Ryo did not seek attention. She did not ask to be believed. She simply shared what she saw, and left the rest to time.

What makes her story so compelling is not just that some of her dreams appeared to come true, but that she dared to document them at all—vivid, unsettling glimpses of futures most of us try to ignore. She offered no explanations, no doctrines, no conclusions. Only visions, stark and mysterious, suspended in black-and-white panels, waiting.

And perhaps that's the heart of her legacy: the space she leaves open. In a world obsessed with certainties and control, Ryo Tatsuki reminds us that not everything must be explained to be meaningful. Some truths arrive in fragments. Some warnings are gentle. Some wisdom wears the face of a dream.

To tell her story has been to walk the borderlands between skepticism and belief, imagination and reality, science and soul. Whether you leave these pages convinced of her prophetic insight or content with symbolic metaphor, I hope you carry forward a deeper sense of humility about what we claim to know—and a greater openness to the unseen currents that shape our world.

For in the end, this biography is not just about a woman who dreamed the future.

It is about a world learning, too slowly perhaps, to listen.

Made in the USA
Middletown, DE
30 June 2025

77688848R10044